D0578122

Louis ★★ SOCKALEXIS
★★ NATIVE AMERICAN BASEBALL PIONEER

by BILL WISE

illustrated by
BILL FARNSWORTH

LEE & LOW BOOKS INC. ★ NEW YORK

It was June 16, 1897. The major league Cleveland Spiders had traveled to New York to play the Giants. Thousands of baseball fans packed the grandstand and bleachers of New York's Polo Grounds. Hundreds more spilled onto the outfield, clustered behind a rope barrier.

Although almost everyone in the stadium had come to root for the home team, people had also flocked to the ballpark to watch a Cleveland Spiders rookie make history. His name was Louis Sockalexis, and he was the first Native American to play major league baseball. This was Louis's Polo Grounds debut.

As Louis trotted out for pregame warm-ups, the air filled with taunting Indian war cries. The New York fans were the wildest he'd seen. Determined to stay calm, Louis doffed his cap to the unruly spectators.

Louis had come a long way from that summer day in 1884 when he first fell in love with baseball. Twelve years old at the time, Louis was standing on a riverbank near his family's home on the Penobscot Indian reservation in Maine. In a clearing beyond the far bank he saw a group of boys from town hitting a ball with a wooden stick. Finally one of the boys noticed Louis and called to him to join the game. Cautious but curious, Louis got into his canoe and paddled across the river.

For the rest of the day, Louis played baseball with the boys. They took turns pitching and catching, hitting and fielding. It didn't matter that Louis was Native American and the boys were white. All that mattered was baseball. Louis was hooked.

When the sky turned dark the games ended and Louis paddled home, weary but content. For a few magical hours, baseball had taken Louis to a special place, away from his everyday life.

Times were difficult for the Sockalexis family. Like other Native Americans, they did not have the same rights as white Americans and were forced to live on a reservation. Money was scarce, and home was a small wooden shack. Louis's father, Francis, worked hard at his two jobs as a logger and a river guide. Francis was also a leader of the Penobscot tribe, and he taught Louis to be proud of his heritage.

Louis deeply admired his father. It was Francis's example that showed Louis the importance of determination, hard work, and pride. Toiling alongside his father, Louis helped chop down towering pine trees for the logging company. Louis didn't mind the physical work, but he preferred to swing a baseball bat, not an ax.

Louis began to throw himself into baseball more and more, playing every free moment. When he couldn't find a game, Louis made his way to the river to practice on his own. To strengthen his throwing arm, he tossed stones as far out into the water as he could. To hone his swing, he threw stones into the air and whacked them across the river with a homemade bat. All the while Louis dreamed of becoming a major league baseball player.

As a teenager, Louis attended a
Catholic high school where sports
were a regular part of the curriculum.
There he grew into a talented
ballplayer. Louis could outhit,
outthrow, and outrun everyone. His
reputation spread, and people from
all over Maine came to watch the
Native American boy play baseball.

Not everyone cheered for Louis
at these games. Often he heard
spectators making fun of him,
shouting out insults. Others pointed
and stared, laughing at "the Indian
playing a white man's game." Deep
inside, Louis was stung by such
abuse, but he decided early on not
to let anyone get in the way of his
dream. With dignity and grace, Louis
fought back by smashing home runs.
On the baseball diamond Louis felt
like a king.

After he graduated from high school, Louis went to Holy Cross College in Massachusetts on an athletic scholarship. With his blazing speed on the base paths, powerful throwing arm in the outfield, and tape measure home runs at the plate, Louis became one of the biggest stars in college baseball.

One day Pat Tebeau, manager of the Cleveland Spiders, came to watch Louis play. When Tebeau saw Louis hit the ball with such power and ease, his eyes lit up with excitement. He offered Louis a contract to play for the Spiders.

Louis was thrilled, but his father scoffed at the news, saying baseball was a waste of time. Francis Sockalexis told his son that his rightful place was on the Penobscot reservation with his people, not traveling the country with a baseball team.

Louis respected his father, but his baseball dream pulled on him until he ached. With a heavy heart, Louis made his decision. He hoped his father would one day understand.

In the spring of 1897, Louis packed his suitcase and boarded a train to Cleveland, Ohio. He was heading for the majors. Sitting quietly in the back of a bustling train car, Louis gazed out of the window. He was proud to be fulfilling his dream, but he never felt more alone.

Life in the major leagues was difficult for Louis. Many of his new teammates didn't want a Native American in the starting line up. Spectators jeered, booed, and shouted racist comments when Louis walked up to the plate. Newspapers were no better, calling him "The Deerfoot of the Diamond," "Chief Sock-em," and "The Savage." Undeterred by this cruelty, Louis courageously carried on. For the first two months of the season, he stunned fans across the country, pounding whatever opposing pitchers threw at him.

On June 16, 1897, the Spiders were at the Polo Grounds in New York, ready to play the Giants. Louis and his team weren't up against any ordinary pitcher that day. Amos Rusie, the man known as the Hoosier Thunderbolt, would be on the mound.

Rusie was a four-time thirty-game winner and five-time strikeout king. Armed with a sizzling fastball and a nasty curve, Rusie was feared by batters like no other pitcher. Four years earlier baseball rules-makers had paid Rusie the ultimate compliment when they moved the pitcher's mound back ten feet in an attempt to curb his blazing fastball. But Rusie still threw fast and hard— so hard that the New York catcher lined his mitt with a sheet of lead so his hand wouldn't split open when he snared one of Rusie's heaters.

Rusie was irritated by all the publicity Louis had been getting around the league. In the days leading up to the game, Rusie made headlines by promising New York sportswriters that he would strike out Louis.

The stadium was packed, and Rusie was cranked for the showdown. It was the top of the first inning, and the Spiders were up. Louis was scheduled to bat third.

After Rusie struck out the leadoff batter and coaxed the second batter to groundout weakly, it was Louis's turn to hit. A wave of excitement rippled through the stands when

Louis grabbed his bat and strode to the batter's box. From all corners of the ballpark, voices rumbled. "Strike the chief out," they shouted. "Get a tomahawk, not a bat!"

Louis took a deep breath and nodded toward the grandstand. Another chorus of war whoops filled the air. The crowd wanted Louis to strike out. They wanted him to realize that baseball was still the white man's game.

The fans rose to their feet and began stomping up and down on the wooden bleachers, yelling at the top of their lungs. The sound was crushing, but all the howling, all the hatred only made Louis more determined to prove that he belonged.

Louis took a moment to scan the stadium. Suddenly, down the left-field line, he saw members of his Penobscot tribe. They had traveled all the way from his hometown to cheer for him. Among the group stood his father. Louis had not forgotten his father's example and his pride in his heritage. Louis was no longer playing just for himself. He was batting for his father and his Penobscot people.

Out in the field, the New York players were ready for action. The infielders hunkered down, steeling themselves for one of Louis's stinging line drives. The outfielders moved back, deeper and deeper, stopping only when they came up against the outfield ropes.

Standing atop the pitcher's mound, Rusie spit into his glove and stared in at Louis. Rusie's lips curled into a frown. The Hoosier Thunderbolt was trying his best to intimidate Louis.

Unfazed, Louis lifted his bat to his shoulder and burrowed his feet into the batter's box. Louis felt powerful and confident. He knew he could hit Rusie's best stuff.

Tension crackled in the air. Louis and Rusie exchanged glares.

Louis fixed his eyes on Rusie, and waited.

Squinting, Rusie peered in at his catcher for the sign. Then he nodded. He was ready to pitch.

The crowd hushed in anticipation. Everyone stood perfectly still.

Rusie went back into his windup. Slowly he twisted and extended. Then, like a catapult, he fired a fastball that whistled toward home plate.

With lightning-fast reflexes, Louis's arms uncoiled. He snapped his wrists and whipped the bat across the plate.

CRR-RACKKK!

The ball blasted from the bat. Rusie spun around to see the ball rocket over the second baseman's head. Steadily the ball rose, gaining speed as it sliced through the air. The right fielder and center fielder didn't even budge. Each one turned his head and watched the ball soar by.

As the echo from the crack of the bat faded in the air, the crowd remained silent. Finally the ball landed over the right-field ropes and disappeared into a sea of Giants fans. The players were frozen in place, staring at the spot where the ball had come to rest. No one had ever seen a ball hit that far in this ballpark.

The stillness of the moment was broken by the motion of a lone figure—Louis Sockalexis—steadily making his way around the bases. There were no more boos or insults from the Giants fans. Instead, the crowd began to cheer. The noise grew louder and louder until it filled the stadium. Rounding third base, Louis peered up into the grandstand in astonishment. The New York fans were doffing their caps in his honor. He had won their respect.

Crossing home plate, Louis looked down the left-field line and nodded to his people. His father nodded back, a proud smile etched on his face.

Once again Louis felt the magic of baseball, just as he had on that summer day in 1884 when the game first took him to a special place. But on this summer day, it was Louis Sockalexis who created the magic and took the game of baseball to its own special place.

Afterword

After his dramatic home run against the Giants in 1897, Louis Sockalexis continued to dazzle the baseball world. As late as July of that year, he was batting almost .400 and was ranked among the league leaders in base hits, triples, stolen bases, batting average, slugging percentage, and runs batted in. This brilliant streak came to an unfortunate halt when Louis broke his ankle. For the rest of the summer, he played through the pain and

COURTESY OF THE COLLEGE OF HOLY CROSS

struggled at the plate. Still, he finished the season with a .338 batting average, one of the highest averages ever by a major league rookie.

Overwhelmed by a career-crippling injury and continued racial hostility, Louis began to battle with alcoholism. His playing time dwindled over the next two seasons, and in 1899 Louis was forced to retire at the age of twenty-seven. With his major league career over, he returned to Maine, later becoming a youth baseball coach and umpire, and working as a logger.

In his brief career, Louis Sockalexis was one of the most versatile players in baseball, amazing everyone who had the chance to see him. At Holy Cross College, he recorded an astonishing .862 slugging percentage in 1895, batted .441 over two seasons, set the United States amateur record for the longest baseball throw (393 feet), and once stole six bases in a single game.

Louis's extraordinary feats earned him a shower of praise from premier baseball experts. National Baseball Hall of Fame legend John McGraw, who managed in the major leagues from 1896 to 1932, called Louis the greatest natural athlete he had ever seen on the diamond. "If Sockalexis had stayed in the big leagues for five years, he could well have been better than Ty Cobb, Honus Wagner, or Babe Ruth," said McGraw. Hughie Jennings, another Hall of Fame manager, wrote, "At no time has a player crowded so many remarkable accomplishments into such a short period of time as Louis Sockalexis. He should have been the greatest player of all time—better than Cobb, Wagner, Nap Lajoie, Rogers Hornsby, or any other of the men who made history for the game."

Being the first Native American to play in the major leagues, Louis paved the way for other Native American and minority players. Shortly after Louis's career ended, star pitcher Charles Albert Bender, standout catcher John Meyers, and the legendary Jim Thorpe—all Native Americans—got opportunities to play in the majors. In 1945, almost fifty years after Louis's rookie season, Jackie Robinson officially broke baseball's "color line," becoming the first African American to join a major league team.

For his playing ability and contributions to baseball, Louis was inducted into the American Indian Athletic Hall of Fame, the Holy Cross College Athletic Hall of Fame, and the State of Maine Baseball Hall of Fame. A courageous man of great pride, Louis Sockalexis was a true American sports pioneer and an inspiration to many.

★ ★ ★ ★

Author's Sources

Anderson, Will. *Was Baseball Really Invented in Maine?* Bath, Maine: Anderson and Sons Publishing Co., 1992.

Fleitz, David. *Louis Sockalexis, The First Cleveland Indian.* Jefferson, North Carolina: McFarland & Company Inc., 2002.

McDonald, Brian. *Indian Summer: The Forgotten Story of Louis Sockalexis, the First Native American in Major League Baseball.* New York: Rodale, 2003.

Porter, David. *Biographical Dictionary of American Sports: Baseball.* Westport, Connecticut: Greenwood Press, 2000.

To Mary Ann, with love—B.W.
To Allison—B.F.

Acknowledgments

Special thanks to John Bear Mitchell, member of the Penobscot Nation and associate director of the Wabanaki Center at the University of Maine, for sharing his insightful knowledge of Penobscot culture.

Notes

In 1915, two seasons after Louis Sockalexis's death, the Cleveland Spiders were renamed the Cleveland Indians. Some baseball historians assert the name was chosen to honor Louis, while others argue that the team simply adopted the derogatory nickname sportswriters used back when Louis wore a Cleveland uniform. Most historians agree that the name was a result of Louis's association with the team. Today many Native American and activist groups lobby to rid the sports world of the offensive use of Native American imagery in team names and mascots.

There are also claims that James Madison "Jim" Toy was the first Native American to play in the major leagues, in April 1887. However, Toy's Native American ancestry has been debated, and due to poor record keeping at the time, it is hard to determine his heritage. It does not appear that Toy was identified as Indian during his baseball career, and he did not face the same racial barriers and hostilities as Louis Sockalexis.

Text copyright © 2007 by Bill Wise
Illustrations copyright © 2007 by Bill Farnsworth

All rights reserved. No part of the contents of this book may be reproduced by any means without the written permission of the publisher.
LEE & LOW BOOKS Inc., 95 Madison Avenue, New York, NY 10016
leeandlow.com

Manufactured in China

Book design by Tania Garcia
Book production by The Kids at Our House

The text is set in Worcester Round
The illustrations are rendered in oil

10 9 8 7 6 5 4 3 2 1
First Edition

Library of Congress Cataloging-in-Publication Data
Wise, Bill.
    Louis Sockalexis : Native American baseball pioneer / by Bill Wise ; illustrated by Bill Farnsworth. — 1st ed.
       p. cm.
    Summary: "A biography of Penobscot Indian Louis Sockalexis, who pursued his childhood love of baseball and eventually joined the Major Leagues, where he faced racism and discrimination with humility and courage as the first Native American to play professional baseball"—Provided by publisher.
    Includes bibliographical references and note.
    ISBN-13: 978-1-58430-269-8
1. Sockalexis, Louis, 1871-1913. 2. Baseball players—United States—Biography—Juvenile literature. 3. Indian baseball players—Biography—Juvenile literature. I. Farnsworth, Bill. II. Title.
GV865.S588W57 2007
796.357092—dc22
[B]   2006017730